Text copyright © Elizabeth Laird 2022
Illustrations copyright © Mehrdokht Amini 2022

The right of Elizabeth Laird and Mehrdokht Amini to be identified as the author
and illustrator of this work has been asserted by them in accordance with
the Copyright, Designs and Patents Act, 1988 (United Kingdom).

First published in Great Britain in 2022 by Otter-Barry Books,
Little Orchard, Burley Gate, Hereford, HR1 3QS
www.otterbarrybooks.com

All rights reserved

No part of this publication may be reproduced, stored in a retrieval system,
or transmitted, in any form, or by any means, electrical, mechanical,
photocopying, recording or otherwise without the prior written
permission of the publisher or a licence permitting restricted copying.
In the United Kingdom such licences are issued by the
Copyright Licensing Agency, Barnards Inn, 86 Fetter Ln, London EC4A 1EN.

A catalogue record for this book is available from the British Library

ISBN 978-1-91307-429-6

Illustrated with acrylic, gouache, collage and photoshop

Printed in China

1 3 5 7 9 8 6 4 2

STORIES OF
Peace & Kindness
FOR A BETTER WORLD

Elizabeth Laird

Illustrated by Mehrdokht Amini

For Iskander, Ilias, George and Fergus – E.L.
To my aunt and uncle, Mehrak and Abi – M.A.

Contents

Introduction — 9

The Dog-Fight — 10
An Oromo story from Ethiopia

Allah Karim — 16
A story from Sudan

True Kindness — 24
A story from Palestine

The Next Sultan — 30
A story from Yemen

The Emir and the Angel — 36
A story from Afghanistan

The Woodcutter and the Lion — 44
A story from Syria

The Nine Princesses of Kashgar — 52
A Uighur story from China

Introduction

Folktales are ancient wonders of the world. They come bounding out of the past as fresh, fierce and funny as when they were first told. They dangle dreams of magic and glory in front of our eyes, and remind us of scary nightmares too. Every nation on earth has its own folktales. They've been told for thousands of years in the ice houses of the north and the grass houses of the south, in cottages, tents and tepees and in the palaces of kings and queens.

There's wisdom in the old stories, and we need it today. Our world can seem like a sad place sometimes, where too many have had to flee from cruel wars. That's why for this collection I've chosen stories that celebrate peace and kindness.

The first tale, *The Dog-Fight*, was told to me by Mohammed Kuyu, a mesmerising Oromo storyteller, as we sat together by the golden fields of Bale in Ethiopia. Its message of reconciliation struck a special chord with me.

Wars, invasions and oppression have torn apart the countries represented in this book, and millions have had to flee to become refugees in foreign lands, but in these stories we find the true heart and character of their people.

I chose *Allah Karim*, the Sudanese story, for its tender message of compassion towards the homeless. It has a lesson for everyone in cities where beggars live on the streets. *True Kindness*, a story from Palestine, celebrates the golden rule of hospitality, which I discovered for myself in the refugee camps of Gaza and the West Bank. The stories from Yemen and Afghanistan, two countries which have suffered deeply from wars and invasions, show how much their people yearn for just and fair leaders and the rule of law. Syria too is a country ruined by war, but *The Woodcutter and the Lion* shows how much ordinary Syrians value kindness in both words and deeds.

The last story, *The Nine Princesses of Kashgar*, is especially poignant. It tells of the courage of the Uighur people, finding a peaceful way to defend themselves against an invading army.

And now – read on!

Elizabeth Laird

The Dog-Fight
A story from Ethiopia

It was a bright day in the highlands of Ethiopia and the thatched roofs of the village houses were steaming gently in the sun.

A woman came to the door of her hut and gave a bone to her son's little dog, but before he'd had a chance to enjoy it, a bigger dog dashed up and grabbed the bone for himself.

A wise old man heard the dogs snarling and came out to see what the fuss was about.

"Someone had better stop those dogs fighting," he called out, "or the boys will start fighting too!"

No one listened.

The children were coming home from school.

The boy who owned the little dog saw what was happening and ran forward.

"Hey!" he shouted at the big dog. "Leave my dog alone!" And he tried to beat the big dog off with a stick. The big dog's owner ran up.

"Stop hitting my dog," he snarled, "or I'll hit you!"

A moment later two boys had thrown down their schoolbooks and were fighting as hard as they could.

The old man shook his head.

"Will someone stop those boys fighting?" he asked. "If they don't, their mothers will start fighting too!"

Sure enough, as soon as the boys' mothers saw what was going on, they began shouting at each other, getting angrier and angrier.

"This is bad," said the old man. "Now the men will start fighting too!"

He was quite right, because when the first woman's husband came home from ploughing his field, he saw another woman hit his wife with her big spoon. He dropped his plough and tried to pull the angry women apart.

The second woman's husband, who was bringing his cows home for the night, saw a man pulling at his wife. He lost his temper and soon the two men were fighting furiously.

"It's getting worse and worse!" the old man groaned. "Those two men belong to different clans, and now their clans will start fighting too!"

Nobody listened to him. More and more men ran up. Now a battle between the clans was raging.

By the time night fell, sixteen men had been killed, eight from one clan and eight from the other.

When they saw what they'd done, everyone was horrified and very sorry.

"What are we going to do now?" they asked each other. "We've started a war. It could go on and on!"

"Go and consult your elders," the old man advised them. "They'll give you their advice according to our law."

So the clans went to see the elders, who sat and talked for a long time.

At last they called everyone together.

"Every man who killed another must give the dead man's family a hundred cows," they said.

The fighting men looked at each other.

"But if we do that, we'll lose everything we have. What will we live on without our cows? Our families will starve."

The old man stepped forward.

"I know the answer to this problem," he said. "Your pride and anger caused all this. If you want to make peace, you have to throw them away."

Everyone turned on him.

"What do you mean, old man?" they said scornfully. "How can we throw away pride and anger? They're things we can't even see!"

"If it's too hard for you to understand, then you must throw away something that you can see," the old man went on. "Your clans each have their own special emblem, your silver necklaces. They're the most precious things you own. Take them down to the river and throw them into the deepest part, where you will never find them again."

Everyone gasped, too shocked and surprised to speak.

"Your necklaces are your pride," the old man went on sternly. "Throw them away, and your pride and anger will sink with them. You'll learn to forgive each other and live in peace."

The clansmen saw that he was right. Each clan brought out its necklace and threw it into the river. The people forgave each other, and from that moment on they never fought again.

And what happened to the dogs who had started the fight? Well, the big dog was given a bigger bone to suit his size and appetite, and he left the smaller bone for the little dog. Their fight was over too.

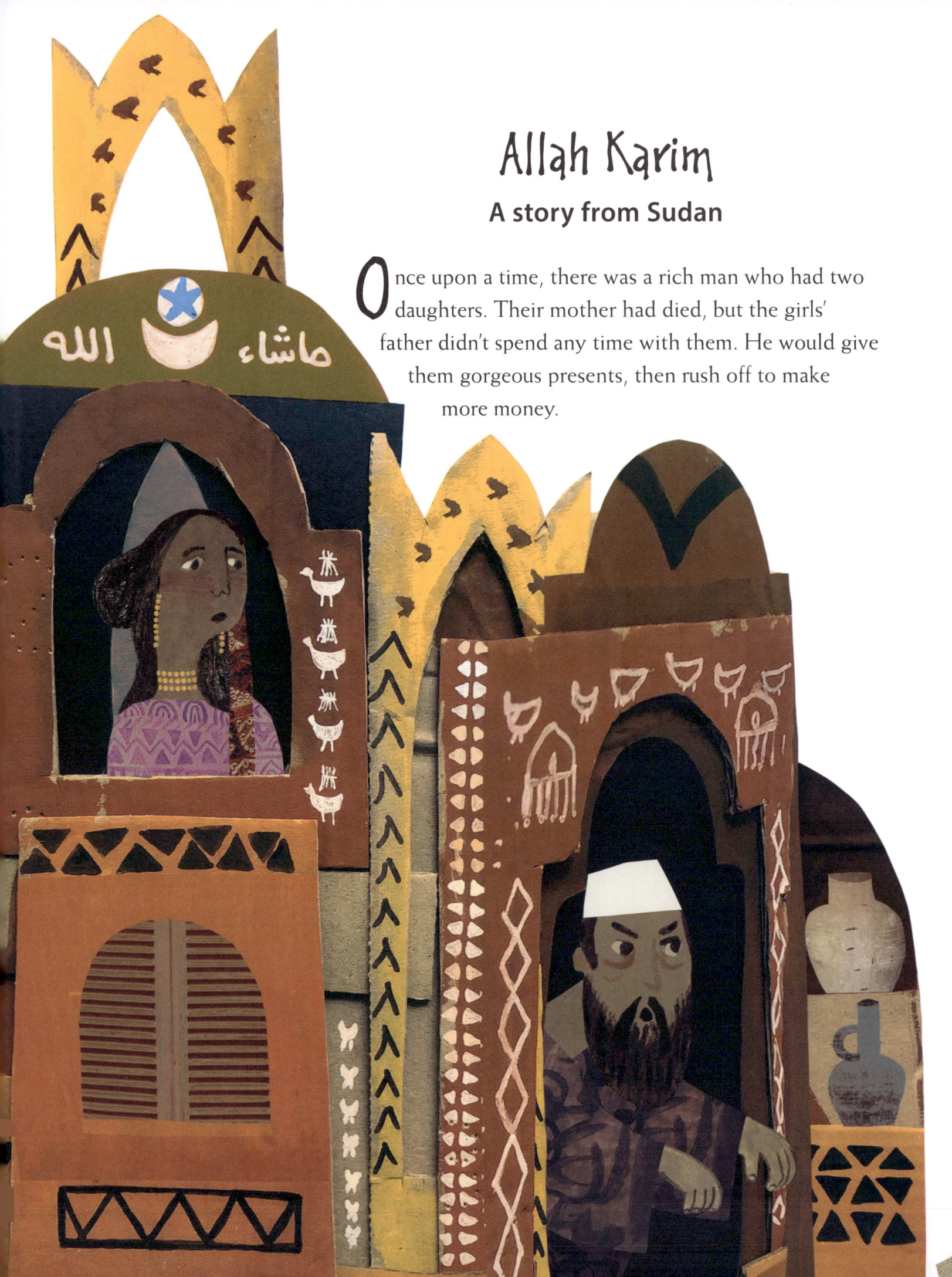

Allah Karim

A story from Sudan

Once upon a time, there was a rich man who had two daughters. Their mother had died, but the girls' father didn't spend any time with them. He would give them gorgeous presents, then rush off to make more money.

The older girl loved her father's presents, but the younger sister didn't want them. She only wanted her father to notice her and love her.

The rich man was annoyed with his younger daughter. He couldn't understand her.

"What's the matter with you?" he demanded. "What more do you want?"

She couldn't answer. She didn't know how to ask for his love.

"You're so ungrateful!" he burst out. "Why don't you put on the expensive clothes I bought for you? That old dress you're wearing is a disgrace!"

"It was my mother's," the girl whispered.

Her father didn't hear. He had whipped himself up into a rage.

"Since you look like a beggar, you shall be a beggar!" he shouted, and he opened the door and pushed her out into the street.

By chance, a beggar was passing by.

"Here's my daughter! You can have her!" the rich man yelled at him.

"What? But I can't look after a girl!" protested the beggar. "I can hardly feed myself and my donkey."

"Allah karim," snarled the rich man. "God will provide."

And he slammed the door shut.

The beggar and the girl looked at each other, too shocked to speak.

"I suppose you'd better come with me," the beggar said at last, and they set off down the road.

They walked and walked, knocking on doors and asking for food. To the beggar's surprise, no one turned them away.

Perhaps she's brought me luck, after all, the beggar thought.

At last they came to the foot of a hill, rising above a town.

"We'll go up there for the night," said the beggar, "where no one will disturb us."

It was a long climb up the hill, and the girl was exhausted when she reached the top. The beggar spread his old blanket on the ground for her, and went back down to the town to beg for their supper. The girl lay down and fell fast asleep at once.

When she woke up, the sun was setting and the donkey had moved away. She led him back and tried to hitch his halter to a stone, but when she touched it, the stone sank into the ground.

"What's this?" she said, looking down into the hole. "Why, it's a jar!"

She pulled the jar out and tipped it over. A river of gold coins and sparkling jewels spilled out on to the blanket!

"Oh!" gasped the girl. "Oh! It's – it's..."

She picked up one priceless treasure after another, then she covered the pile with the corner of the blanket and waited for the beggar to return.

He came back with a bulging sack.

"The people in the town are kind," he told her, opening the sack. "They've given me all this lovely food. Go on. Eat."

"After you," she answered, smiling shyly.

I like this girl, thought the beggar. *I'll look after her as best I can.*

After a while, she asked him, "What would you do if you found a thousand dinars in your pocket?"

"That's easy," laughed the beggar. "I'd feed ourselves for an entire year. There'd be enough for another beggar, too!"

"And if you had two thousand?"

"I'd feed three more beggars. Come on. Why don't you eat your supper?"

"Let's imagine you had a million dinars," the girl went on.

The beggar sighed.

"How wonderful that would be! I'd build a big house where all the homeless people could stay. I'd give them food and medicine and a place to rest and recover."

The girl's eyes shone with happiness.

"Would you really do that if you were rich?"

The beggar frowned.

"Yes, but why are you teasing me with such an impossible dream?"

Laughing, the girl whisked away the corner of the blanket.

"Allah karim!" she said. "God is generous. Look what he has given us!"

Then she told him how she had found the treasure buried in the ground.

The beggar couldn't believe his eyes.

"But it's – it's all yours," he stammered. "You found it. You don't have to stay with a poor beggar any longer. You're so beautiful and kind and rich – you could marry a prince."

"But I want to marry you," the girl said, "and build a home for the homeless right here on this hill."

She persuaded him at last.

The next morning, they hurried down into the town. First they treated themselves to a sumptuous breakfast, then they bought new clothes. After that, they got married, and as soon as that was done they searched out the owner of the hill and bought it from him. They hired masons and carpenters and glaziers, who started at once to build a fine, big house on the very spot where the girl had found the treasure.

When it was finished, they spread the word far and wide that anyone homeless and hungry would be welcome to find rest and safety in the house on the hill.

Their refuge soon filled up, and their family grew too as sons and daughters were born. They all lived together in harmony and happiness.

Now, all this time, things had not gone well for the girl's father. As the years passed, his fortune ebbed away, until he was left with no money at all. His older daughter was ashamed of the poor old man and refused to take him in, so he took to the road and became a beggar.

How cruel I was to my poor little girl, he often said to himself. *This is the punishment I deserve.*

One day, another beggar told him about the house for the homeless, and showed him where it was. The old man was plodding slowly up the steep hill when his daughter looked out through a window and recognised him.

"Quick!" she said to her children. "Bring out the best food for a special guest!"

Her father, exhausted and half-starved, entered the house nervously, half expecting to be sent away. His daughter stayed out of sight, but her children welcomed him and sat him down to eat.

"But this food is fit for a king!" he said.

His daughter came up behind him.

"Allah karim," she said. "God has provided."

Her father knew her voice, and remembered the words he'd flung at her so long ago. He hid his face in his hands with shame.

"Oh, my dearest daughter," he sobbed. "How can you forgive me?"

The girl embraced him.

"Dear Father," she said. "We're together now, and we'll never be parted again. Look, here are your grandchildren, and here is my husband. Allah karim. God has indeed provided."

True Kindness

A story from Palestine

A Sultan was once arguing with his vizier.

"I've noticed something strange," he said. "The very kindest people are the poorest."

"Surely not, sire," said the vizier, taking a sip of sherbet from his jewelled cup. "The poor are stupid and mean. Only rich people can be truly kind."

The Sultan didn't answer, but that evening he called for his chief judge and told him his plan.

The next day the Sultan and the judge dressed themselves as poor holy men, slipped out of the palace without anyone recognising them, and walked out of the city. On they went, mile after mile, until they were far out in the countryside.

At last they saw, down in the valley, a simple hut, where a goatherd was bringing his four goats in for the night. The goatherd looked up and saw the two men. He called out, "It's late afternoon, strangers! Please, come into my house. You can rest here, eat and spend the night."

The Sultan and the judge hurried down the hill. The goatherd welcomed them warmly into his simple hut, then he ran off to his neighbour's house to borrow two loaves of fine, white bread. His wife set them out with some eggs, goat's cheese and olives, and the goatherd begged the visitors to eat.

"Oh, we can't eat this," said the Sultan. "We've made a vow to eat nothing but kidneys for a year and a day."

Without a word, the goatherd went outside, killed his four goats, brought in their kidneys and gave them to his wife to cook. But when the goatherd offered them to his guests, the Sultan said rudely, "We've made another vow to eat nothing before midnight. We'll take the kidneys with us and eat them on the way. And now we'll be off."

The goatherd begged them to stay, telling them how soon it would be dark, how there might be robbers on the road and how they might lose their way, but the Sultan refused to listen.

Once they were back on the road, the Sultan said, "Now we'll try the vizier's house. He's the richest man in the kingdom. Let's see what kind of reception we'll get there!"

There was a party going on in the vizier's house. Light and music streamed from the windows. The Sultan and the judge could smell the delicious food being served to the guests. But when they knocked on the door, the vizier's servants turned them away, and when they knocked again, they heard the vizier shouting, "Get rid of those thieving beggars! Kick them down the stairs!"

The servants obeyed, and the Sultan and the judge were sent flying, landing on the stony path. They got up and staggered back to the palace, covered with bruises.

Next morning, the Sultan called his council of ministers.

"Go with the judge," he said to them. "He'll take you out of the city to a simple shack in the countryside. Tell the goatherd who lives there that the Sultan wants to see him. Ask him to come with you to the palace. You'll find four dead goats by his hut. Bring them with you."

The poor goatherd was terrified when he saw so many soldiers and fine people crowding round his hut.

"What do you want?" he kept saying. "I haven't done anything wrong! And why do you want my poor, dead goats?"

"It's the Sultan's wish," the courtiers told him. "Don't worry. You'll be his honoured guest."

At the palace, the Sultan was sitting on his throne. He was dressed in his kingly robes and looked so different from the ragged holy man of the day before that the goatherd didn't recognise him. The poor man trembled with fear as servants led him up to the seat of honour beside the throne.

The Sultan greeted him kindly, then looked down at the crowd of courtiers.

"You may remember," he said, "a discussion I had with the vizier a few days ago on the subject of kindness."

Everyone nodded and the judge, standing beside the vizier, smiled.

"Good," went on the Sultan. "Now, Judge, tell the vizier about our adventure yesterday."

The vizier's face grew pale and his hands began to shake as he realised that he'd told his servants to kick the Sultan down his stairs.

"You're one of the richest men in the kingdom," the Sultan told him, "but you couldn't even offer a meal to two poor men. This goatherd borrowed fine bread from his neighbour for us, and killed his entire flock of goats, on whom his family depends, even though we were so rude and ungrateful."

The vizier didn't wait to hear more. He crept away, ashamed. The Sultan took away everything he owned and gave it to the poor, while the goatherd, richly rewarded, became his friend and adviser, and sat beside him every day.

The Next Sultan

A story from Yemen

Once there was a Sultan who had three sons. As they grew up, he loved to watch them play. He helped them learn their lessons and he rode out with them to hunt in the desert.

One day he said to his wife, "I'm growing old, my dear, and I think it's time to decide which of our sons will make the best ruler after I'm gone."

His wife didn't like hearing him talk about his own death, but she was a sensible woman so she said, "I couldn't possibly advise you. They're all good boys, and any one of them would make an excellent ruler. Why don't you go and ask the old shepherd who lives on the edge of the Great Desert? You've often said that he's the wisest man in the kingdom."

"That's an excellent idea," said the Sultan, so the next morning he mounted his best camel and rode all day over the sand dunes until, as afternoon turned to evening, he saw a black goat-hair tent in the distance. He urged his camel on and arrived just as the sun slipped down over the horizon.

The old shepherd greeted him warmly and invited him into the tent. His wife, bent low with age herself, made tea for the two men, set it on a tray with a plateful of tasty dates and gave it to her husband. Then she went away to cook a delicious dinner.

After the meal was finished, the Sultan explained to the shepherd why he had come. The old man listened carefully, said nothing for a long time, then gave the Sultan his advice.

I can't see how that would help, the Sultan thought, disappointed. *I've come all this way for nothing.*

But he thanked the shepherd politely, and the next morning, as dawn was breaking, he mounted his camel and rode home.

That evening, he invited his sons to come into the palace's beautiful garden. They sat on silk carpets beside a pool of water, telling jokes and stories, while the moon rose overhead.

After a while, the Sultan remembered the old shepherd's advice.

I might as well try it out, he thought.

He turned to his oldest son and said, "Tell me, which is your favourite animal?"

The young man laughed.

"Is this a game, Father?"

"A kind of game," answered the Sultan.

Without a moment's thought, his son said, "I like dogs best. They're the friendliest of animals. My dogs are always happy to see me. They're loyal and devoted and at night they guard the palace and scare off all our enemies."

The Sultan nodded thoughtfully.

"And you?" he asked his second son. "Which animal do you like best?"

"Monkeys, of course!" laughed the second son. "They're so playful and funny. My pet monkey does the craziest things. Why only yesterday, he stole…"

"Thank you, my dear boy," the Sultan interrupted gently. Then he turned to his youngest son.

"And what about you?"

The youngest prince took his time to answer. At last he said, "I choose the camel."

"The camel?" scoffed his brothers. "It's nothing but a beast of burden!"

"It's much more than that," said the youngest brother. "Think what our camels do for us! We ride them for mile after mile without letting them rest, they carry our merchants' goods, and our armies into war. They give us their milk to drink, and we eat their meat. We make their hides into shoes, and their hair into clothes and tents. They're faithful, but if we treat them badly they grumble loudly and kick us. They teach us to be fair and to look after them properly."

"Thank you," said the Sultan, getting to his feet. "That was very interesting. And now I shall go and say goodnight to your mother."

The Sultana was waiting for him.

"What did the shepherd say?" she asked. "Have you made up your mind?"

"Yes, my dear, I have," said the Sultan. "If our oldest son was the ruler, he'd spend all his time with his friends. They'd do nothing but flatter him and tell him what he wants to hear. He wouldn't learn the truth from them, and they would easily lead him astray. Our second son would spend his time amusing himself with clowns and entertainers. He wouldn't take his responsibilities seriously at all."

"And our youngest boy?" the Sultana said anxiously.

The Sultan smiled.

"He'll make a thoughtful, just and kind ruler," he said. "He'll understand the needs of his people and value everyone in the kingdom."

So the Sultan handed the throne to his third and youngest son, who reigned for many years as a wise and beloved ruler of Yemen.

The Emir and the Angel
A story from Afghanistan

Once there lived a selfish Emir who ruled over a great kingdom. He cared not at all for his subjects. In fact, he squeezed every penny he could out of them in taxes, so that he could buy more gold, more beautiful horses, more sumptuous clothes and dazzling jewels.

All the time, outside the palace walls, his people became poorer and poorer and their children never had enough to eat.

One night, an angel appeared to the Emir in a dream.

"Emir," said the angel. "Why are you making your subjects' lives so miserable?"

The Emir was astonished.

"I'm not making anyone's life miserable!" he objected. "Everyone loves me. Whenever I go outside my palace they bow so low their dirty noses actually scrape along the ground. Why should I care about them anyway?"

"Don't you even know how unjust you are?" demanded the angel. "From now on, be kind and fair to your people. Change your ways before it's too late!"

Then he disappeared.

When the Emir woke up the next morning, he put his dream out of his mind and went off to hunt.

Out in the desert, a gazelle leapt up in front of him. The Emir chased after it, riding so fast that he left his servants, his dogs, his hawks and his hunting cheetahs far behind.

Suddenly, the gazelle disappeared, and a violent wind sprang up. It tore off the Emir's shoes and shredded his fine clothes till they looked like rags. It flung dirt into his eyes and hair. It picked up his horse and hurled it all the way back to the palace stables. The Emir was so frightened that he dropped to the ground and fainted.

When he came round he found himself lying in a tent. A man was looking down at him.

"Who are you?" asked the Emir.

"I'm a shepherd," answered the man.

"Where are all my servants? And my horse?" demanded the Emir.

"What servants?" said the man. "You must have lost your wits. Rest here till you're better."

The Emir shuddered and sat up.

"Stay here? In this humble tent? Don't you know your Emir?" he demanded. "Bow down to me, fool, or I'll have your head cut off!"

The shepherd burst out laughing.

"You? The Emir? That's rich! Look at yourself! Your clothes are in rags, your hair's all matted and full of sand, and you haven't even got any shoes!"

"But I am the Emir," protested the Emir. "And if you don't take me back to my palace at once, I'll… I'll…"

"Take you to the palace? I wouldn't dare!" said the shepherd. "The cruel Emir's guards would never let me near the gates. I can see that the storm's made you lose your wits. Don't worry. I'll look after you."

The Emir had no choice but to accept the kind shepherd's hospitality. Days passed, and when at last the tent was packed up and the shepherd moved on, he took the Emir with him.

A few days later, they came to the city and there, its golden domes glinting in the sun, was the Emir's palace.

"I'm home!" shouted the Emir, running towards the huge gates, without even saying thank you to the shepherd.

The guards leaped forwards to bar his way.

"Stand aside!" roared the Emir. "Your master has returned. Let me in, or I'll have you whipped!"

The guards roared with laughter.

"Get back, you rascal, or we'll throw you into prison!"

"But surely you know me?" pleaded the Emir. "You used to see me every day!"

"How can you be the Emir, when he's right there, in the courtyard?" answered one of the soldiers. "Take a look yourself." And he stood back so that the Emir could see past him.

The Emir started back in horror, because there, sitting on a throne, was a figure who looked exactly like him, dressed in his own clothes. A brilliant, golden light shone round him.

"It's the angel from my dream!" breathed the Emir. "He's taken my place!"

A new life began for the Emir. He had to sleep in doorways and stand with the other beggars when the new Emir came out of the palace to give out food. When his turn came, he looked up with wonder into the dazzling face of the angel.

Everywhere he went, he heard people talking about the change in their Emir.

"The taxes have been cut by half!"

"He listens when people go to him for justice!"

"He helps the sick and the poor!"

"He never used to care how much we suffered. He's like a different man!"

The Emir listened and learned what a bad ruler he'd been.

One cold night, as he shivered in the street, trying to keep warm, he heard shouts from inside a nearby house and saw flames bursting out of a window.

"Help!" screamed a woman. "My children are inside! Someone save them!"

The Emir dashed in through the door, ignoring the flames. He found the children huddling in a corner, lifted them up and carried them out to safety as the house collapsed behind him.

The next time the Emir held out his hands to receive the usual gift of food, the angel smiled at him.

"You did well," he said. "Soon you'll have your reward."

Now the Emir began to notice other people he could help, old men weighed down with heavy loads, travellers needing a guide to show them their way, poor women struggling to push their handcarts through the crowded streets.

They all thanked him and shared with him the little they had – fruit from a market stall, a few coins, fresh bread from the bakery.

"Why did I never know my people before?" he said out loud one day. "How good and kind they are! If only I was their Emir again, how different I would be!"

As soon as he had spoken, the angel appeared in front of him.

"You've learned your lesson," he said to the Emir. "Go back to your old life, and be a fair and kind ruler."

He disappeared, and in the place where he'd stood lay a heap of royal clothes.

Joyfully, the Emir dressed himself and ran to the palace. This time, the guards swung the heavy doors open to let him in.

And from that time on, no one in the Emir's kingdom went hungry, no greedy officials were allowed to steal from the poor, the bullies were punished and everyone who asked for justice received it. Even the cats prowling outside the palace were given their daily milk, and the doves on the rooftop were never without a scattering of corn.

The Woodcutter and the Lion
A story from Syria

Once upon a time a terrible drought hit the land of Syria. Every day people looked up, longing to see a rain cloud, but the sky remained a bright, hard blue. The crops withered in the fields and even the trees lost their leaves and died. Poor people soon had nothing to eat and their lives became harder than ever.

A woodcutter, living in the countryside, spent his days looking for trees to cut down, so that he could carry the wood to the town and sell it for fuel.

After a while, he had cut down all the trees near his home, and no new ones could grow in the hard-baked earth. Every day he returned with nothing and his wife and hungry children had to go to bed without any supper.

Not far away from the woodcutter's village ran the great Euphrates river, and in the middle of it was an island covered in a lush, green forest. The trees there didn't need rain. The river watered their roots.

One night, the woodcutter said to his wife, "Tomorrow I'll row across to the island. There'll be plenty of dead wood lying around. I'll just pick it up and bring it home."

"Dear husband, don't go!" pleaded his wife. "Have you forgotten about the terrible lion that lives there? Haven't you heard him roar in the night? If you set foot on his island you'll never come back alive!"

"But I must find wood to sell soon, or we'll die of hunger," answered her husband. "I'll have to take my chance."

So he picked up his axe and went off to the river.

It was so delightful, walking in the cool shade under the island's trees, that the woodcutter forgot all about the lion. No one had been there for a long time, and branches were lying all over the ground. He was dragging one back to his boat when a fearsome roar made him start with fright.

He turned round. The lion was standing right behind him, his huge teeth gleaming in his mouth and his eyes red with rage.

The woodcutter dropped to his knees.

"Oh sir," he said in a trembling voice. "Have pity on me. My wife and children are almost starving and I can't bear to hear them crying any longer. I beg you, let me take some of this dead wood, so that I can sell it and buy them food to eat."

The lion's heart was touched.

"Very well," he growled. "You may come here once every week and take all the wood you need."

"Oh thank you, th-thank you!" stammered the woodcutter. "I'll never forget your kindness!"

He loaded the boat with wood, sold it in town for a good price, and went home that night with so much delicious food that his family could hardly believe their eyes. They ate and drank in great happiness, and went to bed with their stomachs full.

From now on, every week, the woodcutter collected wood from the island.

"Go on," the lion would say to him. "Take what you need. You are my friend, after all."

"What's that? Oh yes, your friend, of course," said the woodcutter, too busy picking up the next big branch to stop and talk to the lion.

Life was good for the woodcutter now. Everyone needed wood for their cooking fires, and he was the only person who could get it. He employed teams of men, and the lion let them take as much wood as they wanted. The woodcutter set his prices high, and before the drought was over he was a rich man.

He moved his wife and children out of their little, mud-brick house into a fine residence, and they ate roasted lamb, plump dates and honey pastries every night.

One day, the woodcutter decided to throw a party. He hired musicians, prepared a feast and invited all his friends. But he didn't invite the lion.

The smell of delicious food and the sound of happy music wafted across the river to the island. The lion lifted his head, sniffed the air and listened.

"My friend must be giving a party," he thought. "It would be rude of me not to go."

So he brushed his mane, twirled his whiskers, rowed himself across to the shore and trotted up to the woodcutter's house.

The guests scattered in terror at the sight of the lion, but he went boldly up to the woodcutter and said, "How could I stay away from your party? After all, I am your dearest friend."

The woodcutter was embarrassed by his rough, wild guest, and anyway, the lion's breath was so bad that the smell was enough to knock him over.

"Dearest friend?" he scoffed. "Not with your bad breath. Stay away from my guests or you'll make them feel sick."

The lion was deeply hurt. He turned round and slunk back to his island.

The next day, when the woodcutter led his men across the river to cut more wood, the lion was pacing up and down on the shore.

"Go away!" he roared. "And don't come back!"

"Why? What's wrong?" said the woodcutter.

"You turned me away from your party!" growled the lion. "How could you be so rude and ungrateful after all I've done for you? If you'd plunged your axe into my heart you couldn't have hurt me more."

An evil thought entered the woodcutter's mind.

Supposing I do kill the lion? he thought. *The island would be mine, then. I could cut down as many trees as I like and I wouldn't have him bothering me any more.*

So he lifted his axe and swung it at the lion's chest. Roaring with pain, the lion crawled off to hide among the bushes.

The woodcutter claimed the island for himself. He cut down more and more trees and made more and more money. But one day, to his surprise, the lion appeared. He was thinner, older, and with a scar across his chest. He leaped on the woodcutter, pinning him to the ground.

"Get off my island! How dare you cut down all my trees? If you ever return, I'll kill you!"

"But… but…" stammered the woodcutter, looking up into the lion's furious eyes. "I thought we were friends!"

"Friends!" snarled the lion. "You insulted me and attacked me. And I can tell you, my one-time friend, that the wound from your axe has healed, but the cruel words you spoke to me will be in my heart forever."

The woodcutter was ashamed. He crept sadly away.

I've been selfish and cruel, he thought. *I've lost everything now, and the worst thing to lose was my friend.*

The Nine Princesses of Kashgar
A Uighur story from China

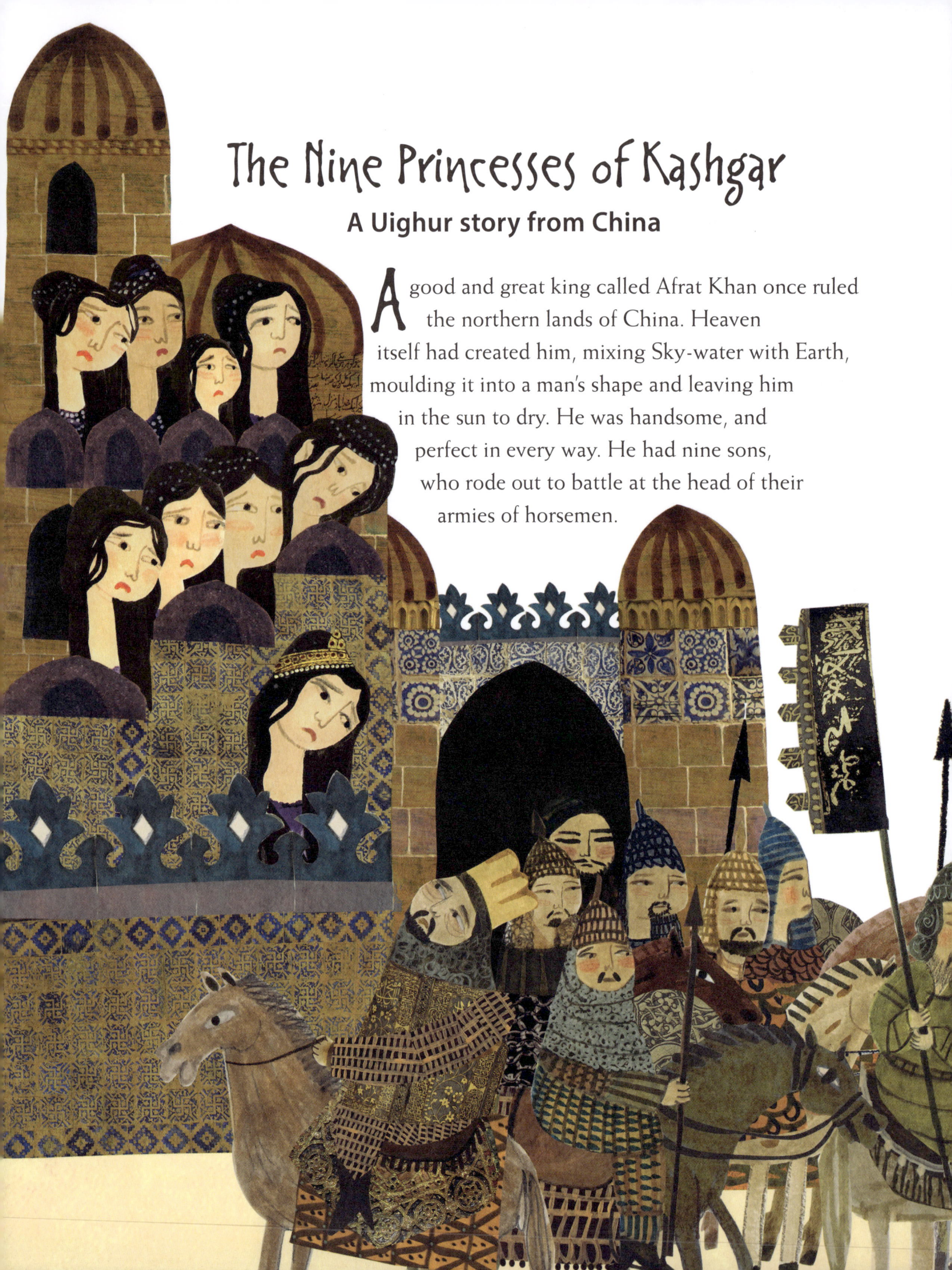

A good and great king called Afrat Khan once ruled the northern lands of China. Heaven itself had created him, mixing Sky-water with Earth, moulding it into a man's shape and leaving him in the sun to dry. He was handsome, and perfect in every way. He had nine sons, who rode out to battle at the head of their armies of horsemen.

One night, Afrat Khan dreamed that the Emperor of Rome, far away in the west, was preparing a huge force to attack him.

The Emperor is powerful, thought Afrat Khan. *He'll easily beat us. I must attack first and take him by surprise.*

He called his sons and gave them their commands. Soon, regiments of cavalry were ready to set off on the road to war. What a sight they were! Their curved swords flashed and their colourful pennants fluttered in the breeze as the horses pranced, impatient to be off.

The Khan called his nine daughters to him.

"I leave my kingdom in your hands," he told them. "Ayhan, my youngest daughter, you're the bravest of all my girls. Build an army of women warriors to defend our country from attackers. I know you'll be fearless in battle and inspire your people to follow you."

Ayhan blushed and courage flooded her heart.

"Kan Kiz, my oldest girl," Afrat Khan went on. "You'll take my place and rule here in Kashgar. Be kind to all our people. Look after the poor and sick. Treat everyone with respect."

Kan Kiz's eyes glowed with pride at the confidence her father showed in her.

The Khan's eyes swept over his other daughters. One he chose to be the Prime Minister. The others he made officers of the city guard. Then he looked up at the forests that bordered his kingdom and called out,

"Forests, preserve my kingdom and my daughters from storms!"

He turned to the mountains, and cried, "Mountains, you're the strongest of all! Bless my people with life!"

Off rode the Khan, with his nine sons and his great army, but as they wound through a high mountain pass, a storm broke out, a river suddenly flooded and he and his whole army were swept away.

Not one man survived.

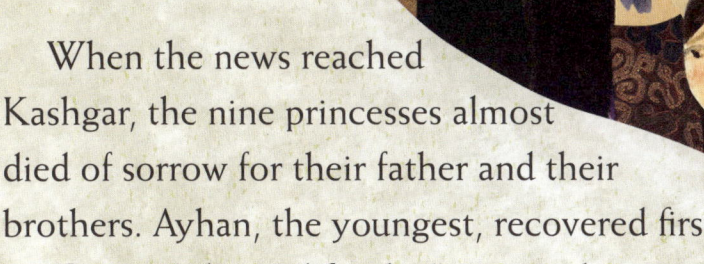

When the news reached Kashgar, the nine princesses almost died of sorrow for their father and their brothers. Ayhan, the youngest, recovered first.

"Sisters," she said firmly, "we must be on our guard. We're alone now and all our country's enemies will think we're weak. They'll come to attack us."

She had hardly finished speaking when a messenger ran in.

"Princess, I heard the Khan of Yaka laughing at the thought of women in charge of a country. 'We'll defeat them easily,' he said, 'and Kashgar and all its riches will be ours.'"

Ayhan frowned.

"It's as I thought," she said. "We can't hope to defeat Yaka Khan in battle. He's not even a man, but a demon in human form. If we try to fight him, our women warriors will be killed, and who'll look after our children? We'll be a nation of orphans. No, we must choose peace and put all our efforts into defending ourselves."

"But how?" Kan Kiz asked her.

"The Sandy Queen of the Desert will advise us," said Ayhan. "She's a Wise Woman who has the power of magic."

The Sandy Queen listened carefully to the anxious young princess.

"What can we do?" Ayhan asked her. "Should we build a great wall?"

"No," the Sandy Queen replied. "Yaka Khan will easily break through a wall. It would be better to bring the sandy desert in to surround Kashgar. It may not halt the demon Yaka Khan, but it will slow him down."

The women started work at once. Led by the nine princesses, they carried bag after bag of sand from the desert and laid it around the city.

"This is hopeless, Ayhan," Kan Kiz said to her sister. "Look how little sand we've brought in, even with all of us working together." But Ayhan wouldn't listen.

"We must carry on," she said.

The Sandy Queen, watching from far away, was impressed by the girls' courage. She called up her magic powers, and under the princesses' astonished eyes, she sent the dunes of the great desert rolling around the city in rippling, golden waves.

Yaka Khan set off to attack Kashgar. His horses floundered in the soft sand, but still they advanced, while Yaka Khan climbed a hill and, with his demon powers, tried to call up a storm to destroy the city.

The forests heard him.
"Afrat Khan prayed to us," came a whisper from the leaves.
"We'll take the strength out of the wind."
"You, forest, can't stop me! I'll make a hurricane!" bellowed Yaka Khan.
But the mountains heard him.
"Afrat Khan prayed to us for life," they rumbled.
"We'll block the path of the hurricane."
Yaka Khan raged against the mountains, but they stood firm.

"Water will bring me victory!" stormed Yaka Khan.

He commanded the sea to rise and flood the city of Kashgar, but the women dug deep channels to divert the water, which sank into the sand and drained away.

At last Yaka Khan knew that he was defeated. He pulled back his armies and left the women of Kashgar alone.

Now peace came to Kashgar, but wise Ayhan knew that other enemies would come one day.

"The desert has been our friend and saviour," she told her sisters. "From now on we'll build our cities in its oases and around its edges. The sand will keep our enemies away."

Peace brought happiness to Kashgar, but Ayhan never stopped mourning for her father. She rode out sometimes into the desert, crying, and calling to Heaven to send blessings on her family and her country. If you should ever go to the great desert near the city of Kashgar, you might hear Ayhan crying. The people who live there now may not remember her courage and wisdom, but somewhere in their hearts she lives,
and will do so forever.

Source Notes for the Stories

The Dog-Fight
Narrated to Elizabeth Laird by Mohammed Kuyu
Asasa, Ethiopia, 1998
adapted from www.ethiopianfolktales.com/oromia

Allah Karim
Adapted from *Egyptian and Sudanese Folktales* by Helen Mitchnik,
Oxford University Press, 1978

True Kindness
Adapted from *Folklore of the Holy Land* by JE Hanauer,
Duckworth, 1907

The Next Sultan
Adapted from *The Land of Sheba* by Carolyn Han,
Interlink Books, 2005

The Emir and the Angel
Adapted from *Tales of Afghanistan* by Amina Shah,
Octagon, 1982

The Woodcutter and the Lion
Adapted from *Syrian Folktales* by Muna Imady,
MSI Press, 2011

The Nine Princesses of Kashgar
Adapted from *Uighur Stories from Along the Silk Road* by Cuiyi Wei and Karl W Luckert,
University of America Press, 1988